MW01201648

To

Mom

Love
From

Daphne

Date
May 13

2012

WHEN YOU NEED
AN
Angel

ROBERT D. LESSLIE, MD

HARVEST HOUSE PUBLISHERS

EUGENE, OREGON

WHEN YOU NEED AN *Angel*

Text copyright © 2012 by Robert D. Lesslie, MD

Published by Harvest House Publishers
Eugene, Oregon 97402
www.harvesthousepublishers.com

ISBN 978-0-7369-3722-1

Photographs used with permission from the following sources:
Masterfile: cover and page 1 • Alamy Images: pages 7, 47
Getty Images: used throughout the book as background imagery • iStockphoto: page 20
Shutterstock: pages, 4, 10, 16, 22, 28, 32, 34, 39, 40, 42

Design and production by Left Coast Design, Portland, Oregon

Printed in China

12 13 14 15 16 17 18 19 20 / FC / 10 9 8 7 6 5 4 3 2 1

This book is dedicated to the men and women who are described in these pages. Their lives and hearts reflect the love of Jesus Christ and the transforming presence of the Holy Spirit. It is my honor and privilege to tell their stories.

Contents

Preach the Gospel at all times and when necessary use words.

SAINT FRANCIS OF ASSISI

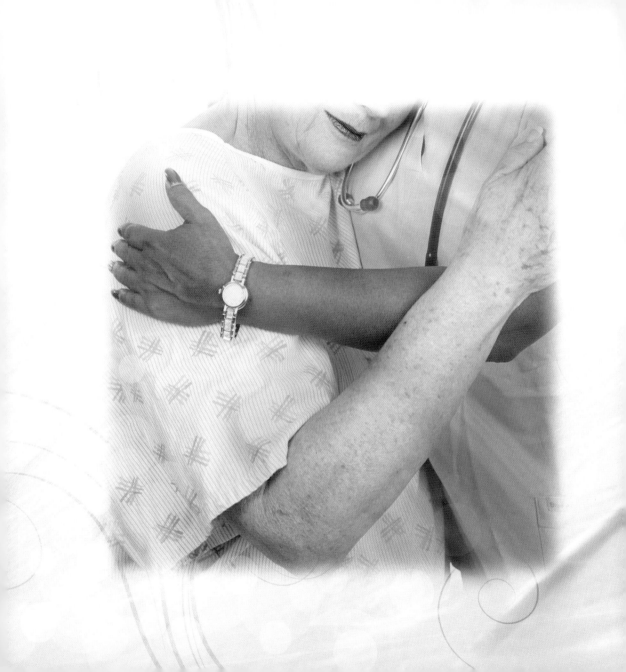

In the Twinkle of an Eye

Do not forget to show hospitality to strangers,
for by so doing some people have shown
hospitality to angels without knowing it.

HEBREWS 13:2

If you don't believe in angels, spend some time in the emergency room.
You will soon learn angels do in fact exist, and they manifest themselves in
a variety of forms. Some are nurses, a few are doctors, and many are
everyday people, passing through our doors and into our lives.

Lori, one of the nurses, pushed Macey Love through the triage door in a wheelchair. Macey was leaning forward and tightly gripping the handles of the chair.

"We're going to five," Lori said. "It's her asthma again."

Macey saw me and smiled, nodding her head. She was struggling for breath, and I could hear her wheezing from across the room. "I'll be right there," I told Lori. To another nurse I said, "Give Respiratory Therapy a call and tell them Macey is here."

Macey Love was well-known to the staff of our emergency department. She was a sixty-two-year-old woman

who had suffered with asthma all of her life. Over the past decade or so, the disease had worsened, necessitating frequent visits to the ER. Usually we could turn her asthma attacks around without admitting her to the hospital for an overnight stay. She made her feelings perfectly clear on that point. "Dr. Lesslie, I've got to get back home and take care of my two grandchildren, so you'd better get me tuned up," she would tell me.

The two girls, eight and ten years old, had been living with Macey since their mother abruptly left six years ago. They were neat kids, friendly, smiling, and well-behaved. It was easy to see that Macey was proud of them, and they loved her dearly.

Lori was starting the IV when I walked into room five. After listening to Macey's chest, I stood back and looked down at her. Before I could say anything, she raised her hand and shook a finger at me. "I know. I know, Macey," I said. "We'll do everything we can to keep you out of the hospital. But you're pretty tight this time. You know that."

She nodded and smiled as Lori fitted a mask across her mouth and nose to deliver a vaporized concoction of oxygen, water, and a bronchodilator.

Macey knew the routine and started sucking the misty medicine as deeply into her lungs as she could. As I told her what was to happen next, she continued smiling.

It was the smile that always struck me. More than just a simple pleasant smile, Macey's started with a twinkle in her eyes and seemed to make her glow. It didn't matter how sick she was; she was always smiling.

To the soul, there is hardly anything more healing than friendship.

THOMAS MOORE

Virginia Granger had been affected by that smile for more than fifty years. They met as young girls in the 40s and became fast friends. Although their grade schools were segregated, they managed to see and play with each other on a regular basis. But after finishing high school, Macey took a job at a local dry-cleaning establishment, and Virginia left Rock Hill to realize her dream to become a nurse. For years they hadn't seen each other.

Then one night several years ago, while Virginia and I were working, Macey walked into the ER in the midst of a severe asthma attack. The two recognized each other immediately, and Virginia quickly set to work caring for her dear friend.

As I entered the exam room, I heard Macey say, "Ginny, I'm just so glad you're here today to take care of me. You know," Macey continued between her gasping respirations, "the Lord has blessed me mightily. He truly has."

She paused to catch her breath, and I listened carefully, curious as to how she would continue the thought. She was in the ER, in significant distress, and suffering from a disease that was not going away. And yet she spoke of being blessed.

I would soon learn about the blessings of Macey Love. She told us about her granddaughters, she reminded Virginia about her loving Father, and she told us of her complete lack of fear as she faced her failing health. In the midst of all of that was her smile…and those twinkling eyes.

On this particular visit, Macey responded to our treatments, and I was planning to send her home in an hour or so. I walked over to room five to let her know this. When I pulled the curtain back, I saw a smiling Macey look up at me. Virginia was sitting by her side, and she too glanced up as I entered and then looked back at Macey. They were holding hands.

I stood there for a moment, watching these two women, these two friends. "I'll be back in a few minutes," I stammered and backed out of the room.

Although Macey is gone now, I can see her face as clearly as if she were in the room with me. I will never forget that smile, those twinkling eyes, and the special feeling we all experienced in her presence.

The writer of the book of Hebrews advises us to always be hospitable, lest we be in the presence of an angel and not realize it. With Macey, I knew. With Virginia, I was certain.

Devoted

Let us run with perseverance

the race marked out for us.

HEBREWS 12:1

Our lives can change directions in a hurry, or sometimes the bend in the road is gradual, barely noticeable at first. Either way, at the end we're faced with hard realities and even harder decisions. To be able to stay the course, to run the race, requires a strength beyond our own.

The first time, I didn't know.

John Miller came into the ER with a pretty bad burn. It wasn't anybody's fault. Some hot coffee had accidentally spilled on his right forearm and caused a second-degree burn. It had blistered almost immediately and should have been causing some pain. But as he lay on the stretcher, he didn't seem to feel much of anything, and if he did, he wasn't minding it.

Helen, his wife, sat dutifully by his side, patting him on the shoulder and reassuring him with soft, soothing words. John just smiled and nodded his head.

He was seventy-nine years old and in remarkably good health, all except for the distant, empty look in his eyes.

John was obviously suffering from some sort of dementia.

"Am I hurting you?" I asked as I trimmed away the charred and dead tissue on his arm.

He just looked at me, smiled, and nodded his head.

"He's fine, doctor," Helen said. "You just do what you need to do. I can tell that he's not hurting."

Helen was a few years younger than her husband, but not by many. Tall and slim, she had made it a habit to exercise regularly and stay healthy. She watched closely as I finished cleaning her husband's burns.

"There, that should do it for today," I told them, "but we need to recheck him here sometime tomorrow."

"That will be fine," Helen answered. "About this time? Will that be suitable?"

"That will be great," I told her. "I'll be here so ask for me. I'd like to recheck him myself."

Helen gathered their things, and the two made their way slowly down the hallway and outside. Her footsteps were strong and sure. John's were shuffling and awkward.

As they disappeared through the automatic doors, I turned to Lori, the nurse who had assisted me, and said, "That's really tough. She's an angel carrying quite a load."

"You don't know their story?" she asked, an edge of unbelief in her voice.

"What story?" I replied, wondering what she meant.

John Miller and Helen Fisher had grown up in Fort Mill, a small town just south of Charlotte. Their parents were friends, and both families attended the same downtown church. Despite a slight age difference, the two were inseparable from grade school on. Their parents approved and watched their budding puppy love grow deeper as the years passed.

When Helen was a sophomore cheerleader, John starred as a senior on the football and basketball teams. They were high-school sweethearts. When the time came for John to consider where he would attend college, the reality of a separation became painfully clear. Promises were made before John headed off to Clemson to study engineering.

For a while, letters passed between them with faithful regularity. Summer vacations and the long Christmas breaks gave them a chance to spend time together.

Then Helen made plans to attend the University of Virginia in Charlottesville.

Though they both were bothered by the distance between the two schools, they spent that summer declaring their love and making promises to wait for each other until after they graduated from college.

But as so often happens, time and distance took their toll. Letters arrived less frequently, and their vacation plans just didn't seem to mesh. John went on to grad school, where he met another engineering student. Helen met a young man from Roanoke.

"They just went their separate ways, married others, and had children," Lori told me. "It apparently surprised a lot of people in Fort Mill because they seemed to be the perfect couple. I think John lived in Asheville most of those years, and she was somewhere up in Virginia, maybe Roanoke.

"Then a few years ago, John's wife died. With their two grown children living on the west coast, John was left alone living in the mountains of North Carolina. A few months later, Helen's husband also died, leaving her by herself in Virginia. Their three sons lived in the Charlotte area.

"Somehow they reconnected," Lori continued. "She said it was as if the fifty years in between had never happened. Within a couple of months, they were married. It was a storybook ending," she said, smiling.

> *The golden moments in the stream of life rush past us and we see nothing but sand; the angels come to visit us, and we only know them when they are gone.*
>
> GEORGE ELIOT

"But the happily-ever-after didn't last very long. Within a year of rekindling their relationship, John began to lose things, wander off in the neighborhood, and have careless, clumsy accidents. The progression of his Alzheimer's disease was relentless and rapid. In less than a year, he was unable to take care of himself, and Helen, try as she might, reached a point where they were both in danger if she didn't get some help.

"She made the decision to have him moved into a long-term care facility, one experienced in taking care of people with dementia," Lori explained.

"That must have been a hard choice for her," I said, struck by the painful irony of their story. "I mean, to find each other again after all those years and then to be—"

"To be separated again?" Lori finished my sentence. "That wasn't going to happen. Helen made arrangements with the retirement center, and she moved in with John. She sold her house and everything. She told me it was an easy decision, and the support of all their children made it even easier."

"Hmm," I murmured, "I didn't know."

The next day, Helen brought John back to the ER. His burn looked good. "Let's check him a couple more times," I told Helen, "and then the staff at the center should be able to handle it."

She thanked us while John just smiled.

Lori and I stood at the nurses' station as the couple once again walked out of the ER and into the sunlit afternoon.

"They are really something," Lori spoke quietly.

Where you go I will go, and where you stay I will stay.

THE BOOK OF RUTH

Joshua

Praise Him all creatures here below.

THOMAS KEN, "THE DOXOLOGY"

C.S. Lewis tells us that "people need more to be reminded than to be instructed."
The Lord reminds us of what's essential in many ways. Sometimes it's through the lips
of little children—and sometimes through the wonders of His creation.
In the ER, as in all of life, it's important to step back,
take a deep breath, and be reminded.

Sally Jefferson was far more mature and wise than her eight years. Developing insulin-dependent diabetes at the age of three had forced her to grow up pretty fast. Yet this difficult disease had not dimmed her enthusiasm for life, her lively sense of humor, or her genuine empathy for the feelings of others.

"Thanks, Jeff," she whispered, listless and glassy-eyed but still managing to somehow smile at the nurse sitting beside her stretcher.

"Gonna be a little stick…" he said to her softly, not wanting to hurt her. He quickly inserted the IV, allowing fluids to run in.

"That wasn't bad," she told him, smiling.

Glancing at her watch, Sally's mother looked over at me and asked, "Do you think she'll need to be admitted this time, or is there a chance we can go home in a while?"

It was almost four in the afternoon. If everything went well, she might be able to get home by eight or nine. After I told Mrs. Jefferson this, Sally quickly looked at her mother and frantically asked, "What about Joshua?"

"Don't worry about Joshua, honey," she told her daughter. "We'll make sure he's taken care of."

"But, Momma…" Sally pleaded.

"Who's Joshua?" I asked, curious about what made her so upset.

Sally looked up at me with her large brown eyes and said, "Joshua's my miniature donkey. He needs to be fed and watered tonight. Daddy's out of town, and there's nobody at home."

"I didn't know you had a mini. How old is he?"

Sally's face brightened as she began to tell me about Joshua.

Her grandfather had decided it was time for Sally to learn how to take care of other living things. He had heard miniature donkeys were good animals, social and even-tempered. And so, on a bright spring Saturday morning, the two had traveled over to Clover and picked out Joshua, a one-year-old gelding.

"Out of all the donkeys, Joshua picked me," Sally said, nodding her head. "He's my best friend."

"I know what you mean," I agreed. "I have one too."

She looked at me wide-eyed and asked, "You have a donkey?"

"Sure do," I told her. "His name is Atticus, and he's about five years old now."

While her IV fluids ran in, we talked about our donkeys and how much fun they were.

Then with a surprising maturity evident on her face and in her voice, she looked back at me and said, "I think Joshua is like Jesus."

The simplest things—a gentle word, a soothing touch— bring joy and peace like summer rain.

DINAH MARIA MULOCK CRAIK

This took me completely by surprise. "Now that's an interesting thought," I told her. "Tell me what you mean."

"Well, it's just that when I'm out in the pasture with Joshua, just the two of us, it's like I'm there with Jesus." She stopped and shook her head in frustration. "I don't know… It's hard to explain."

"Please, Sally," I encouraged her, "I want to hear about that."

She looked up at me and, with a small sigh, started once more. "First of all, he's gentle and kind. And he's patient. That's one of the most special things about him. He's always waiting for me to come out to see him. Sometimes he'll holler at me just to remind me he's there, but then he just watches and waits. And when I go to him, he's always glad to see me. He's always quiet and calm, and he loves me no

matter what—even when I'm in a bad mood, or tired and angry, or in trouble with Momma and Daddy.

"Every time I'm with him, I feel better. I feel happy. He's a lot bigger than I am, but he's always careful when we're together. I'm never afraid around him. He makes me feel safe…just like Jesus."

The three of us sat in silence for a moment, and I marveled at this little girl's insight and wisdom. I believed Sally was right about Joshua—and Atticus too. She was describing our pets far more eloquently than I would ever be able, and in ways I had never considered.

"Thanks for sharing that with me, Sally," I said quietly. "That's a lot to think about. Are you sure you're only eight years old?"

"Eight and a half," she answered, smiling.

Sally stayed in the ER with us for a couple of hours and then was able to go home with her mother.

As I left the hospital later that evening, I thought about what Sally had said about her donkey, and I thought about Atticus.

I drove home to our property and directly to his fenced pasture. There he was standing in the middle of the field quietly looking at me. I parked the car, walked through the barn, and saw that he was already heading in my direction. We met face-to-face. He looked up at me with his huge, gentle eyes. Sally's words surrounded us, and for a moment, we just gazed at each other. I reached out and put my arm around his neck. We stood side by side, breathing quietly and watching the last of the sunset settle beyond the distant pine trees.

We were happy and at peace. And I knew I needed to be more like Him.

The Greatest Virtue

All people are like grass, and all their
faithfulness is like the flowers of the field.

ISAIAH 40:6

Twenty-five years in the ER have taught me a lot of things. I know without a doubt that life is fragile. I have come to understand that humility may be the greatest virtue. And I am convinced we need to take the time to say the things we deeply feel to the people we deeply care about.

The two sisters were in their eighties now. They lived in one of our town's older neighborhoods, in the house their father built so long ago. Sarah Gaithers was a retired schoolteacher, but Emma had suffered some unspecific accident during her delivery and had never developed normally or held a job. Emma's mental age was about three or four years, and her legs were twisted and useless, as was her left arm and hand. She was able to use her right hand, but she had never developed any significant dexterity. After her mother and father died, she had been totally dependent on her sister.

Sarah assumed this responsibility unflinchingly. She never married and considered Emma the focus of her life. As of late, Sarah was having a more difficult time taking care of her sister. While Emma did not have any chronic medical problems, Sarah had developed diabetes and hypertension. In spite of her dedicated and indomitable spirit, she was growing weaker.

"Come along this way, Sarah," I heard Lori say. I looked across the room to see Lori transferring Emma from her wheelchair onto a stretcher.

Sarah looked up as I approached. "Good afternoon, Dr. Lesslie. Good to see you," she said to me while holding

Emma's alpaca sweater in her hands, gently smoothing the worn garment over her forearm—a sweater in the middle of July.

"Hello, Sarah," I answered, meeting her eyes and then looking down at her sister. "What's the problem with Emma today?"

"Emma was having her bath, and I was getting her out of the tub. I guess my strength just gave way and she slipped. Her forehead struck the edge of the tub, and…well, you can see what happened," she explained, pointing to her sister's forehead.

Emma was smiling vacantly at me while Lori cleaned her face. As always, I wasn't sure how to respond. Sarah would say that she recognizes us, but I've never seen any evidence of that.

After gently examining Emma's wound, I turned to her sister and said, "She'll need some stitches, probably quite a few. Has she acted like anything else was hurting her?"

"No, other than that she's fine," Sarah responded. She would know. To my knowledge, Emma had never uttered a word. Yet she and Sarah communicated in some unspoken way. If Sarah said she was okay, that was enough for me.

"Good," I said. And then I noticed a small but brilliant sparkle of light in the middle of Sarah's left eye. "Sarah, I thought you were going to get that cataract fixed," I said with feigned sternness.

"Dr. Lesslie, how am I supposed to have eye surgery? Who will take care of Emma? I just don't have the time right now. Maybe…maybe in a couple of months or so."

"Sarah," I gently scolded, "how are you going to take care of Emma if you can't see?"

We had been down this road before, and we both knew there was no good solution to the dilemma.

The only time I had ever known Sarah to demonstrate anything resembling anger was the night Emma fell out of bed and Sarah brought her to the ER. After examining Emma carefully and determining that no serious damage had been done, my young partner, Jack, took Sarah aside and said, "Your sister is going to be all right tonight. She's all right *this* time. But what about the next time she falls…or what if something worse happens?" He then proceeded to tell Sarah that it was time for Emma to be placed in a home where she would be properly taken care of.

Sarah's face had flushed, and her back had stiffened. "Doctor, you don't know me," she had firmly declared, "and you don't know my sister. We have been together for more than eighty years, and nothing is going to change that. I will take care of Emma for as long as the good Lord allows me to."

She paused here and leaned close to his face. "And that, young man, will be His decision and not yours."

She stepped back, collected herself, and then softly said, "I should be getting Emma home now. Thank you for your help."

Several months earlier, Sarah—with Emma at her side—arrived at the ER complaining of a cough, fever, and shortness of breath. We had quickly determined she had a severe case of pneumonia and would need to be admitted to the hospital.

"Dr. Lesslie, that will be impossible," she had told me, shaking her head. "I cannot stay in the hospital. Who will take care of Emma?"

I again explained the seriousness of her situation. Still she refused to be admitted, and I knew I could not force her. Exasperated, I left her room.

After Nurse Virginia listened to my predicament, she abruptly stood up, straightened her starched, pleated skirt, and said, "Dr. Lesslie, give me a couple of minutes with Sarah." After talking to Sarah, she went straight to her office and closed the door. Several minutes later, when she walked out of her office, she was smiling.

"Well, here's the situation," she began. "The administration has agreed to let Emma stay on a cot in the room with Sarah. The staff on the medical floor will make sure she's fed and taken care of. Sarah should be all right with that, don't you think?"

I didn't know what to say. This kind of thing just didn't happen in this hospital. But it did that day...and for several more. After a week of aggressive therapy, Sarah and Emma were once again on their way home.

"Okay, Emma, let's get your fore-head taken care of." I spent the next forty-five minutes suturing her lacera-tion. Sarah stood by her side holding her hand, and all the while Emma just stared at the ceiling, smiling.

"There, that should do it, I said, taking off my gloves.

A few minutes later, Sarah pushed Emma's wheelchair up to the nurses' station and said, "Thanks again for all your help." She patted her sister's shoulder and added, "And Emma thanks you too."

Truly here was a ministering spirit, an angel passing through this life and touching ours.

Every heart that has beat strongly and cheerfully has left a hopeful impulse behind it in the world, and bettered the tradition of mankind.

ROBERT LOUIS STEVENSON

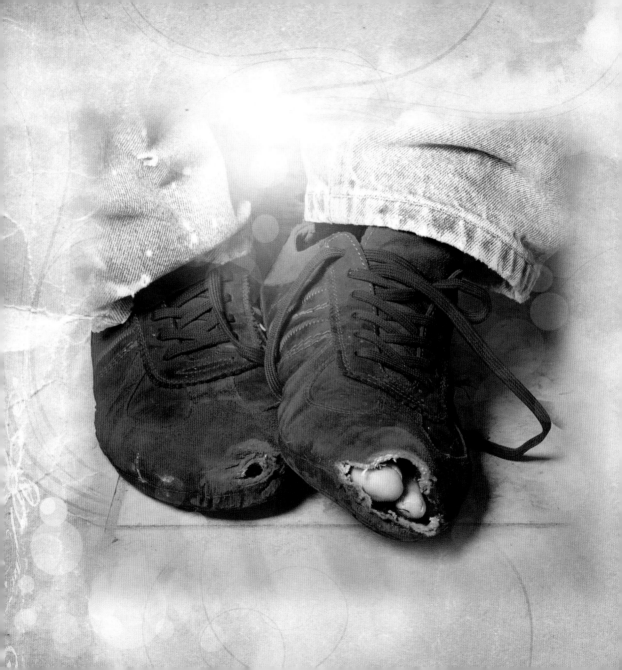

The Least of These

I was hungry and you gave me something to eat, I was

thirsty and you gave me something to drink, I was a stranger

and you invited me in, I needed clothes and you clothed

me, I was sick and you looked after me...

MATTHEW 25:35-36

The ER is a lot of things to a lot of people, but one of its most important
functions is to serve as a safety net for those who have nowhere else to go.
The ER offers the best and last chance some people have for medical care.
Sometimes it's the only place they have for care of any kind.

It was two in the afternoon on a cold, clear Tuesday in February when I heard Denton's voice on the ambulance telephone.

"Medic one, this is Dr. Lesslie. Go ahead," I responded.

"Dr. L, we're bringing in a sixty-five-year-old man with abdominal pain." There was a momentary pause. "It's Slim."

Lori—a quiet yet confident nurse with a compassionate heart—walked over to the nurses' station with a clipboard in her hand.

"We've got a friend coming in," I told her.

"Slim?" she guessed, placing the board in its rack.

"Yep," I answered, "again."

"I'll get Slim's room ready," she told me.

Achieving the exalted status of "ER regular" requires a significant effort. At any given time, we probably have only ten or twelve people in that circle. Our regulars come to the ER again and again with generally the same complaint. It might be abdominal pain, alcohol-related issues, back pain, or seizures. Each has developed their own unique handle.

Slim Brantley had chosen abdominal pain as his handle. Or maybe it had chosen him. Although too much alcohol and three packs of cigarettes a day had taken their toll on his lungs and heart, his stomach was fine. But he used it as his free pass to the ER. In short order, it usually got him a bed and a warm meal. After an hour or two, he would feel better and be ready to go home.

With Slim we tried everything—social services, charity organizations, and on many occasions detox. We even had him committed to a mental hospital once, but nothing worked. It was never very long before he ended up back on the streets and in the ER.

Today Slim seemed especially un-kempt.His clothes were layered for the cold weather. He had on two pairs of trousers; the outermost were stained and torn. His black boots were well-worn and, surprisingly, they matched, but he had no socks. He wore two light-blue sweaters, the outer one at least two sizes smaller than the inner.

Under this was what appeared to be an umpire's jersey.

"Doc, can you give me somethin' for this pain? It's worse than ever!"

I examined Slim, asking him where he had been staying, when the pain had begun, and whether there were any associated symptoms. Convinced nothing serious was going on, I said, "Slim, your belly checks out okay. Do you think if you had something to eat, you would feel better?" Somehow I knew the answer to this question.

There are moments in life when the voice of a friend can sound like a choir of angels to the heart.

AUTHOR UNKNOWN

Slim began to rub the hollow that was his stomach. "Well, Doc, ya know, that would probably do me a lot of good. The pain seems to have eased a little."

I pulled the curtain closed behind me and walked over to the nurses' station to ask the unit secretary to call down to the cafeteria and see if they could send up a tray for Slim.

"It's already on its way—" Amy replied, "a double." Like me, Amy had helped take care of Slim for years.

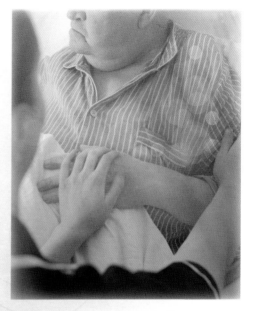

Thirty minutes later Slim was eating. He was quiet and content. The department had gotten busier, and I hadn't checked on him in a while. As I walked past Slim's curtain, an offensive odor stopped me in my tracks. "Not again!" I said toward the nurses' station.

One of Slim's major problems was the development of an untimely loss of bowel control. Untimely because it

A friend loves at all times.

THE BOOK OF PROVERBS

would occur in our department right after he had eaten. To his credit, he was always apologetic.

My thoughts were cut short by the sound of the ER doors bursting open. Two paramedics hurried a stretcher toward the cardiac room, and I followed.

After the heart patient was cleared, I headed back to the nurses' station to write up my report. As I passed by Slim's room, I caught a glimpse through the partially opened curtain.

Lori was in the room with Slim. Gloved, she was cleaning him up… and smiling at him. "Slim, it's all right," Lori said. "Accidents happen. And I'm just glad you're feeling better." Despite the terrible odor, she gently finished the chore.

As she stepped toward the curtain to exit, she paused. She reached out, put her hand on Slim's shoulder, and patted it tenderly. "Slim," she said softly, "you need to take better care of yourself. You need to stop your drinking."

"I know, ma'am. I know. It's just hard," he responded, "but I'll try."

"Good, Slim. That's all we want you to do. Just try."

She'd had this conversation with him before, and yet Lori was still offering her support, again demonstrating that somebody cared about him.

She then turned from the stretcher, but as she did so, Slim caught her wrist. Lori stopped and looked down at him.

"Lori." It was the first time he had ever used her name. "Thanks."

She looked at Slim for a moment and then nodded. He let go of her wrist, and she walked out of the room. She came up to where I stood and stopped, realizing I had been watching. A little color came to her face. No words were spoken. She just smiled, nodded, and walked away.

I remember this particular day well and Lori's unflinching care for Slim. She had gone beyond what was required of her in this unpleasant circumstance and had demonstrated her genuine and selfless spirit. I've tried to do the same.

Doxology

Oh Lord, support us all the day long,

until the shadows lengthen and the evening comes,

and the busy world is hushed, and the fever

of life is over, and our work is done.

THE BOOK OF COMMON PRAYER

All of us lead busy—if not feverish—lives. In our haste,
we chase the unimportant, we fail to appreciate the
significant, and we "miss the forest for the trees."

I had read the patient's chief complaint from his chart for the third time and was still puzzled.

"Leukemia. Need my dog."

Amy looked up, noticed my confusion, and said knowingly, "You'll see, Doc. It threw me for a loop too."

With no time to waste, I picked up the chart and headed to room four.

James Timberland was sixty-eight years old and had been diagnosed with leukemia a few months ago. He lived alone on a few acres of land just outside of town.

As I walked into his room, he looked up from his newspaper and took off his reading glasses. Smiling, he said, "Doctor, I want to apologize

for being here this morning. I know you have emergencies to take care of. I usually go to my doctor's office once a week for my transfusions, but this morning, well, I feel like my blood must be pretty low, and it's the weekend, and…"

I stepped close to the stretcher and put a hand on his shoulder to quiet him. "Don't apologize for being here, Mr. Timberland. You're in the right place, and we're glad to help you."

A brief examination confirmed his fears. His blood pressure was low, his pulse was up, and we needed to get a transfusion going.

"Looks like you're going to be with us for a couple of hours," I explained, making a few notes on his chart. "Is there anyone we can call for you?"

"No, it's just me," he answered quietly, "for the last fifteen years."

When I heard that, I looked up from his chart and into his sad eyes.

Suddenly bright excitement replaced his sad expression, and he said, "Wait! There's Doxology!"

"Doxology?" I asked.

"Yes! He's my golden retriever. He's out in my truck."

James's tired and wrinkled face softened as he continued. "Is there any way he could come in here with me? I mean, if I'm going to be here for a few hours, I'd like… He's not used to being away from me, and he might get worried."

I glanced down at his chart and now understood. "Need my dog."

"Mr. Timberland—" I began.

"I'm James," he corrected me.

"James, I'll see what I can do, but right now we need to get you taken care of. Someone from the lab will be down in a few minutes, and Lori, one of our nurses, will be right in."

"He's almost fourteen years old," James explained, "and he doesn't hear so well anymore—doesn't see too well either—but just rub his ears and tell him, 'You're gonna go see Poppa.' He'll come right along."

I was smiling as I walked back out to the nurses' station—until I saw Virginia, our head nurse, staring straight at me.

"What's this about a dog?" Virginia asked sternly. "Come with me to the medicine room," she directed, leaving no latitude for negotiation or explanation.

As we walked into the small space that overlooked the parking lot, Virginia stepped over to the window and silently stared out across the pavement. "See that pickup truck?" she asked, nodding in the direction of an old blue Ford. "That the dog?"

I located the truck and saw Dox, alert and attentive, sitting behind the steering wheel. He seemed to be staring straight at us.

"No dogs allowed in this hospital," Virginia stated flatly. "Rules." She looked directly at me and said, "I'll be in my office—with the door closed." Then she left the room.

James had been right. As I approached the truck with its windows down, Dox didn't bark at all. I leaned close, rubbed his ears, and said, "Let's go see Poppa." He flicked his tail and slowly got up on his feet. We unhurriedly made our way to the ambulance entrance and down the hall to room four.

I thank my God every time I remember you.

THE BOOK OF PHILIPPIANS

Three hours later, with Dox lying comfortably on the floor near his stretcher, I told James, "If you're feeling up to it, we'll help you on your way."

"Dox and I are ready to get back home, Dr. Lesslie, but have you got a minute?" he asked.

"Sure," I said, glancing at my wristwatch. "What is it?"

Folding his arms across his chest, James said, "You know, doctor, I haven't had much to do for the past couple of hours except lay here, talk to Dox, and look around this room. It strikes me that you folks are pretty much tied down."

Curious, I pulled up a stool and sat down. Dox looked up at me, slowly wagged his tail, and then set his head back down on the tiled floor. "What do you mean?" I asked.

"Well, just look around," he said, motioning with his hand. "There's a clock on the wall measuring each minute, my heart monitor beeping and

measuring my heart rate, and the IV thing. It's clicking away, measuring out the last little bit of blood I need. Everything is measured and counted out, every minute, every hour, and every day. Just look at your wrist," he said, glancing at my watch.

I felt a pang of regret, wondering if he had seen me sneak a look at my watch when he had asked me to stay.

"I'm sure you work a set number of hours here," he continued. "I wager that an alarm clock woke you up this morning and you'll set it again tonight.

And tomorrow the whole thing will start again." He paused and looked at me, waiting for a response.

He was right, of course, but I didn't know what to say. I just nodded my head.

"The real danger is when days turn into months and then into years—and then they're gone." He sighed deeply and glanced over at his IV.

"Look at Dox. He has no idea what time, what day, or what year it is. He's just living and enjoying every minute, happy to be with the ones he loves. That's the way I'm going to live for the time I have left. I'm going to free myself as much as I can from alarm clocks, calendars, and schedules—and especially watches," he added, winking at me.

A little while later, I watched Lori carefully push James Timberland in a wheelchair to his truck. Dox swaggered slowly behind them.

Then I picked up the next patient's chart and immediately glanced at the clock on the wall. Suddenly, with a painful and heavy realization, I realized James was right. I *was* tied down— and by too many things. True, my job required me to focus on seconds, minutes, numbers, and measures. Yet I knew what James had said was important. He had figured it out—he and Doxology—and I needed to figure it out too.

Angels promote closeness and foster tenderness.

AUTHOR UNKNOWN

Wonders and Mysteries

We are like children, who stand in the need
of masters to enlighten us and direct us; and God
has provided for this, by appointing his angels
to be our teachers and guides.

THOMAS AQUINAS

The ER is a difficult and challenging place to be, both for patients and for those of us who care for them. Yet the same pressures and stresses that make this place so challenging also provide an opportunity to experience some of life's greatest wonders and mysteries.

The ambulance doors opened, and Willie's two daughters wheeled him into the ER. One of them looked up at Virginia and me and said, "It's Daddy's heart again. He's havin' trouble breathin'."

"Having some trouble tonight, Willie?" Virginia asked, stepping between the two women and taking control of the wheelchair. "Let's just head over this way," she added as she looked at me and nodded in the direction of the cardiac room.

Willie James was sixty-three and had suffered a pretty significant heart attack three years ago. Since then he had teetered on the edge of heart failure.

Tonight Willie was calm—he even managed to smile at Virginia—but he was too short of breath to answer any questions.

Willie was wearing an old T-shirt and well-worn plaid trousers. He wore no shoes, and his socks were tattered and dirty. I followed him and Virginia into the cardiac room. Glancing at the clock on the wall, I noted the time— ten thirty-five.

We were all thankful when, at last, Willie's condition began to improve. Even so, he needed to be admitted to the hospital.

"Willie, isn't Angus Gaines your doctor?" I asked, making sure that only a movement of his head was required for a response.

He nodded in affirmation.

"Good. I'll give him a call and tell him you're here."

Angus Gaines was in his early seventies and still practiced medicine full-time. He had been in Rock Hill for more than forty years, and while technically a general practitioner, he took care of just about everything. He didn't do any surgery now, but he had more patients than any other physician in the area. He would want to know Willie was in the ER, and I knew he would want to see him.

To Angus it didn't matter what time of day or night we called. Within a matter of minutes, he would arrive. I had never heard him utter a cross word or show any sign of frustration with his patients for being called so late at night. This night was no different.

The nurse handed the phone to

There are persons so radiant, so genial, so kind, so pleasure-bearing, that you instinctively feel in their presence that they do you good, whose coming into a room is like the bringing of a lamp there.

HENRY WARD BEECHER

me. "Angus, this is Robert Lesslie in the ER," I said, wondering if we had woken him up. "I've got one of your patients here—Willie James. He's in congestive heart failure again."

"Willie James, you say." The gravelly voice sounded in my ear. Angus seemed wide awake. "Does he live at 122 Bird Street? And he was born, uh, sometime in April of 1930, right?"

I looked at Willie's chart. "Yep, that's right." I was always amazed at his good memory. It occurred to me that a large part of his motivation for remembering these things was the genuine care he had for his people.

"Okay, yeah, I know Willie. I'll be over directly."

When the ER doors hissed open and Angus walked in, the clock showed twelve twenty-two. It had been just eleven minutes since I had hung up the phone.

As Angus walked past the nurses' station and toward the cardiac room, I could see that he was wearing a knee-length charcoal coat over his pin-striped pajamas. On his feet were brown leather bedroom slippers. He took off his gray derby hat and tossed it onto the countertop.

I gave him a brief update as he pushed open the door and we stepped into the room. Willie and his daughters looked in our direction as we entered. You would have thought it was Christmas morning by the way their eyes lit up and smiles spread across their faces when they saw Dr. Gaines. One of the daughters ran across the room and hugged him. "We're so glad you're here!" she said.

Thirty minutes later they left to check him into the hospital. As Angus picked up his hat at the nurses' station, he turned to me. "Thanks for looking after Willie. I'm just going upstairs to make sure he gets settled in. I'll have one of the cardiologists come and take a look at him too."

The rest of my shift was uneventful. I grabbed my briefcase and walked out the doors at five till seven. The early morning air was clean and cool, and the sun was trying to peek over the trees at the far end of the doctors' parking lot.

As I walked up the hill toward my car, my attention was drawn by some movement behind and to the left of me. I stopped to look. I saw the figure of a man dressed in a dark overcoat and derby hat. It was Angus Gaines. He was just now leaving the hospital, having spent the entire night in Willie's room, unwilling to leave his side until he knew that Willie was going to be all right.

His hands were thrust deep into his pockets, and he shuffled along in his bedroom slippers, obviously deep in thought. And then something strange and amazing happened. A single beam of early morning light made its way through the trees to shine directly on this remarkable man.

Silently one by one,

In the infinite meadows of heaven,

Blossomed the lovely stars,

The forget-me-nots of the angels.

Henry Wadsworth Longfellow